A Little Welsh Cookbook

E. Smith Twiddy

ILLUSTRATED BY DELYTH JONES

First published in 1990 by
The Appletree Press Ltd,
19-21 Alfred Street, Belfast BT2 8DL
Tel: +44 232 243 074 Fax: +44 232 246 756
Copyright ' 1990 The Appletree Press Ltd.
Printed in the E.C. All rights reserved.
No part of this publication may be reproduced
or transmitted in any form or by any means,
electronic or mechanical, photocopying,
recording or any information and retrieval
system, without permission in writing
from the publisher.

First published in the United States in 1991
by Chronicle Books, 275 Fifth Street,
San Francisco, CA 94103

ISBN 0-87701-858-8

9 8 7 6 5 4 3 2 1

Introduction

The homes of Wales – the Land of Song and Welcome in the Hillsides – traditionally had kitchens that fed princes and paupers alike. This small collection of Welsh recipes are gathered from every corner of Wales from the remote hill farm areas of Snowdon to the bustling seaside towns of Cardigan Bay and from the old country estates to the dark coal-mining valleys of the South. Wales is famed not only for the herring and mackerel catches that fill the ports, and the sweet salmon and trout of the calm rivers, but also for its succulent mountain lamb and fresh country herbs. Welsh food is as wholesome and hearty as is the *'Croeso'* (Welcome) that you will receive on the hearth of every Welsh home. I hope that these recipes will give as much pleasure to the cook and the reader as they gave the author in their collecting.

A note on measures
Metric, imperial and volume measurements have been given for all the recipes. For perfect results use one set only. Metric measures should be used where no American measure is shown, as for meat weights. Spoon measurements are level except where otherwise indicated. Seasonings can of course be adjusted according to taste. Recipes are for four.

Cawl

Traditional Welsh Soup

Traditionally this was a meal in itself, but is now a soup course and a lunchtime dish in Welsh restaurants today. Like many Welsh recipes, the soup varies slightly according to what is available at the time. Originally kid meat was used, a residue from the days when wild goats roamed the densely-wooded hills.

---

1 lb/500 g bacon pieces
4 large potatoes
4 carrots
1 leek
2 onions
small piece of swede
knob of butter
1 tbsp flour
salt and pepper
meat stock to cover

Peel and cut the vegetables. Melt butter in a large saucepan and add vegetables with flour to coat. Brown slightly then add meat and seasonings. Cover with the stock and simmer until cooked. Leave to cool and then skim any fat off the top. Serve with warm crusty bread or parsley dumplings.

Parsley Dumplings

4 oz/125 g/1 cup self-raising flour
2 oz/50 g/¼ cup suet
good pinch of fresh parsley
enough water to mix

Mix well and shape into dumplings. Add to soup and cook for 5 minutes. Serve immediately.

Glamorgan Sausages

In his book of Welsh travels in 1862, *Wild Wales*, George Borrow wrote that the Glamorgan Sausages he had for his breakfast were just as good as the famed Epping Sausages.

½ lb/250 g/4 cups fresh white breadcrumbs
½ lb/250 g/2 cups onions, finely chopped
1 large egg, beaten
1 egg, separated
pinch dry mustard
pinch fresh herbs
oil for frying
flour, salt and pepper

Mix all the dry ingredients together. Add beaten egg. Whisk the egg white until stiff. Shape the sausage mix into long shapes. Dip in the egg white then coat with flour. Fry in hot fat until browned. These sausages contain no meat and are suitable for vegetarians.

Ffest y Cybydd

Miser's Feast

This dish was so called because of an old man who lived in Cardiganshire and who died a very wealthy man. Rumour had it that he saved his money by eating the meat on Monday, the vegetables on Tuesday, and drinking the soup on Wednesday. A miserly tale indeed, but apparently true.

---

1 piece of lean bacon
4 large potatoes
½ swede or turnip
2-3 leeks
½ lb/250 g carrots
3-4 medium onions, sliced
light stock to cover
salt and pepper

Cut up meat into small cubes. Chop vegetables. Arrange in a fairly shallow dish in alternate layers of vegetable and bacon. Season and pour over the stock. Cover and bake for about 1½ hours at gas mark 5-6/375°F/195°C.

Golwythen o Borc

Tenderloin of Pork

Most cottagers kept small livestock such a pig, a cow, a milking goat and a few chickens for their own use. On a 'high day' the pig would be killed and this dish made with the choicest cuts of pork. The children were given the pig's bladder blown up to make a football.

---

2 tenderloin fillets 1-1½ lb/500 g
Stuffing
4 oz/125 g/½ cup finely-shredded suet
8 oz/250 g/4 cups white breadcrumbs
8 oz/250 g sausage meat
⅓ pint/200 ml/¾ cup water
salt and pepper
4 oz/125 g/⅔ cup cold stewed apples
large pinch chopped parsley
handful of sultanas
1 tsp thyme

Mix all the ingredients together and spread the stuffing on one fillet. Cover with the other fillet and tie together with string. Cook for approx. 45 mins at gas mark 4/350°F/175°C.

Katt Pie

Mutton Pie

These pies were often served newly-baked at the November Hiring Fairs.

Pastry
1 lb/500 g/4 cups plain flour
½ lb/250 g/1 cup suet
pinch of salt
enough water to make a dough

Filling
1 lb/500 g lean mutton
¼ lb/125 g/⅔ cup currants
2-3 large onions
salt and pepper
2 tbsp brown sugar
stock to moisten

Make the pastry and line one large dish or six small ones. Mince the mutton, chop onions, and add to the currants and sugar. Season and moisten with stock. Fill the cases and cook for 30-40 mins at gas mark 6-7/400°F/200°C.

Gwydd Rhost

Roast Goose

Goose has always played an important part in Welsh rural life. Only recently has its place been taken over by turkey at Christmas. The goose down was used for pillows, eiderdowns, and feather mattresses. The large wing pinions were used to sweep the hearth and the smaller ones to sweep the tables.

---

1 goose, 9-10 lbs/4-5 kg
Stuffing
4 oz/125 g/2 cups breadcrumbs
2 medium-sized onions, finely chopped
large knob of melted butter
½ oz/2 tbsp/1½ cup chopped parsley
6 oz/175 g/1 cup cooked gooseberries
1 egg

Add beaten egg to the first six ingredients and mix. Either stuff the goose with this, or cook it separately. Cook goose at gas mark 4/350°F/180°C for 20 mins per lb and 20 mins over.

Ffagotts

In the past nearly every cottager kept a pig and this dish was created from pig meat that could not be used for any other purpose.

---

8 oz / 250 g streaky bacon, minced
8 oz / 250 g pork belly, minced
8 oz / 250 g pigs's liver, minced
4 oz / 125 g / 2 cups fresh white breadcrumbs
2-3 medium sized onions, finely chopped
salt and pepper
good pinch dry mustard
6 oz / 175 g / 1 cup stewed apple
1 large egg, well-beaten
2 good pinches of chopped parsley
2 oz / 50 g / ¼ cup suet

Mix the meats together with the suet. Add the breadcrumbs, onions, salt and pepper, mustard and parsley. Add the apple pulp and egg. Mix well. Shape into 4 ffagotts and place on a baking dish. Cook at gas mark 6-7 / 350°F / 175°C for 45 mins until well browned and the meat is cooked through.

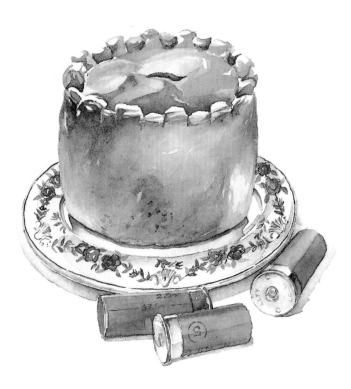

Pastai Helgig

Game Pie

Pheasants and deer were bred on large estates. Gamekeepers were kept busy trying to keep local poachers at bay and preventing them from helping themselves to the game. Records show that at least one Welsh man was transported to Australia for poaching in the early 1800s.

---

1 lb/500 g shortcrust pastry
1 lb/500 g venison, hare, pheasant and pigeon (boned and chopped
¾ lb/400 g bacon pieces
½ pint/300 ml/1¼ cups jellied stock (made from game bones)
½ oz/10 g/1½ tsp gelatine
salt and pepper
good pinch ginger
egg yolk to glaze the pastry

Line a loose-based round cake tin with foil and then line the base and sides with pastry. Put a layer of bacon pieces on the bottom and the other meats on top. Add seasonings, then pour in half the stock. Cover with a pastry lid and glaze top with egg yolk. Make a slit in the pastry top. Cook at gas mark 4-5/375°F/190°C for about two hours. Allow to cool. Dissolve the gelatine in 3-4 tbsp hot water, add to rest of stock, heat gently but do *not* boil. Pour the jellied stock into the pie through the slit. Chill the pie for several hours. Cut into slices.

Hunter's Stew

The meats used in this stew were often given to the poor farmworkers by their masters instead of monetary payment. More often, however, they found their way to dinner tables by way of the poacher.

½ lb / 250 g shortcrust pastry
½ lb / 250 g young pigeon breasts
¼ lb / 125 g lean bacon
¼ lb / 125 g lean rabbit meat
½ lb / 250 g hare meat
½ lb / 250 g / 1⅓ cups apples
2 large chopped leeks
stock
salt and pepper
knob of butter
large pinch of flour

Cut the meats into small pieces and toss in the flour. Heat butter and cook meats until browned. Season to taste and leave to cool. Cover the bottom of a pie dish with the leeks and then a layer of apples. Add meats and stock. Cover with a pastry lid. Make a slit in the top and cook for about 10 mins at gas mark 7-8 / 400°F / 200°C, then reduce

temperature slightly and cook for a further 50 mins until all the meats are cooked.

Cig oen Cymraeg

Welsh Lamb

Welsh lamb is reputed to be the sweetest of meats. It is certainly a popular choice on menus, and the small white dots on the mountainsides are proof that there are more sheep than people in Wales!

---

1 leg of lamb
handful of fresh rosemary
Mint sauce
handful of fresh mint
good pinch sugar
white wine vinegar

Cook the lamb sprinkled with rosemary, gas mark 7-8/380°F/180°C for 15 minutes per pound. To make mint sauce, mix mint and sugar with vinegar and allow to infuse for an hour or so. Serve the lamb with fresh mint sauce and roast vegetables.

Leek Pie

The leek is the Welsh National Emblem and traditionally this pie was made on important festival days, such as St David's Day on 1 March. Originally it was called Kettle Pie and in the 1800s the three-cornered leaf which is a type of wild garlic was used instead of leeks.

½ lb/250 g shortcrust pastry
1 lb/500 g/⅔ cups cleaned chopped leeks
8 oz/250 g chopped bacon
5 fl oz/200 ml/¾ cup single cream
3 eggs
salt and pepper
pinch of nutmeg

Line a pie dish with the pastry. Pour all the ingredients into the dish and bake for 40 mins on gas mark 6-7/350°F/180°C.

Pastai i Bwthyn

Cottager's Pie

This is a complete meal made in one dish. It was often put in the 'ffwrn' or oven, and left to cook slowly all day when the cottagers were out at work in the fields. It filled hungry mouths when families were large and incomes were small.

½ lb/250 g shortcrust pastry	½ pint/300 mls/1¼ cups milk
1 boiling fowl	salt and pepper
4 onions, sliced	good pinch flour for thickening
4 carrots, diced	
10 potatoes, sliced	pinch nutmeg
8 thick slices of bacon	butter for frying
handful of fresh parsley	

Take the meat off the fowl. Heat the butter in a large fryingpan then add the meat, onions and carrots. Sprinkle with flour and brown slightly. Add seasonings and nutmeg. Cook for a few minutes. Transfer to an ovenproof dish. Place potatoes over the top and add the milk. Cover with the pastry case. Glaze with milk. Bake at gas mark 5-6/375°F/180°C for about an hour until vegetables are cooked and the pastry is brown. Sprinkle the top of pie with the chopped parsley before serving.

Eog

Salmon

The Teifi and Dovey rivers vie for which has the best salmon in Wales. Salmon has a delicate flavour and needs simple cooking and subtle creamy sauces. Traditionally coracles were used for salmon fishing. Made from hide in the past, these small round boats are now made from tar-coated canvas. Nets were put between two coracles and the fish caught in the nets.

---

4 salmon cutlets
1 small carton single cream
2 oz/50 g prawns
salt and pepper

Steam salmon cutlets over boiling water for about 8 minutes or until the flesh flakes easily with a fork. Gently warm cream, seasoning and prawns together and pour this sauce over salmon.

Llyswennod Perlysiog

Spiced Eels

Eels are plentiful around the Swansea coast and this is one way of serving them.

---

3 lb / 1 ½ kg conger eel
½ cup white wine vinegar
6 cups water
salt and pepper
6 whole cloves
1 tbsp fresh basil

Get the fishmonger to gut the eel and chop off the head. Slit the eel open and remove the backbone. Sprinkle with the seasonings both inside and out. Make into a round shape and tie with string. Put the vinegar and water into a large pan. Bring to the boil then drop in the eel. Simmer gently for about 45 minutes. Let it cool in the water. Lift out when cold and cut into slices before serving.

Scadan

Fishguard Herrings

Welsh fishermen went out in all weathers to make their fish catches and their nets were always full. The Fishguard area is still famed for its herrings and this is one delicious way of serving them.

---

8 herrings
2 medium-sized onions, finely chopped
vinegar
10-12 black peppercorns
parsley
salt and pepper
6 small bay leaves

Remove heads, clean and scale the herrings. Slit open and lay flat on a board. Place some chopped onion on each slice. Roll up, starting at the head end. Secure with a toothpick. Place in an ovenproof dish. Season and cover with the vinegar and water. Sprinkle with the bay leaves, parsley and peppercorns. Bake at gas mark 6-7/350°F/175°C for 1-1½ hours. Serve hot or cold.

Bara

Bread

Baking bread is considered an art still very much alive in Wales. Visiting an old bakery will reveal a dazzling array of loaves all of which are named after the locality from which they originated. Baking was done once a week in the old stone oven, and then kept in a wooden crate suspended from the ceiling to prevent the mice getting to the bread.

3 lb / 1.5 kg / 12 cups of ½ white / ½ brown strong flour
1¾ pint / 1 ltr / 4 cups lukewarm milk and water, mixed
1 oz / 30 g fresh yeast
good pinch salt
good pinch brown sugar
knob of melted butter

Mix yeast and sugar. Make a well in the flour and add the yeast mix, salt, liquid and butter. Mix well, then knead for a few minutes. Shape into 4 round loaves and leave to prove in a warm place for about one hour. Bake at gas mark 7-8 / 400°F / 200°C for 45-50 minutes.

Bara Brith

Speckled Bread

This tasty fruit loaf is made from ingredients that are always in the cupboard. It has many variations. It is served as a filling snack at any time in a Welsh home and farmers often take some in their lunch box when they go up the mountain to gather the sheep for shearing.

1/3 pint/250 ml/1 cup strong cold tea
4 tbsp marmalade
6 oz/175 g/1 cup sultanas
Soak the above ingredients for an hour and then add:
8 oz/250 g/1 cup brown sugar
3/4 lb/425 g/3 cups self-raising flour
2 beaten eggs
good pinch mixed spice

Mix the ingredients well and put into a greased loaf tin. Bake for 1½ hours or until cooked at gas mark 5/300°F/150°C.

Cacen Gneifio

Shearing Day Cake

The exotic fruits on top of the cake were possibly goods
brought by smugglers who used the small coves around
the Welsh coasts to land their booty. The locals were
asked to safekeep the booty until the excise men were off
the smugglers' trail.

½ lb/250 g/1 cup butter
½ lb/250 g/1⅓ cup brown sugar
1 lb/500 g/3½ cups self-raising flour
good pinch ginger
2 tbsp brandy
3 eggs
¼ lb/125 g/¼ cup slivered almonds
¼ lb/125 g/¼ cup mixed peel
1¼ lb/625 g/3½ cups sultanas
12 whole brazil nuts
12 whole cherries
2 tbsp apricot jam

Cream sugar and butter. Add beaten eggs, ginger and
flour. Mix well and add brandy, fruit and nuts. Bake at gas
mark 4/300°F/150°C for about 2 hours until well
cooked. When cold arrange the brazil nuts and cherries in
a cluster on top of the cake. Melt about 2 tablespoons of
apricot jam and pour over the nuts and cherries.

Cacen y Glowr

The Miner's Fruitcake

Mid-Wales had a network of lead mines and this cake was made for the lunch or 'tocyn' boxes of the men and small boys who worked in the mines.

---

8 oz/250 g/1 cup dripping
1 lb/500 g/4 cups self-raising flour
8 oz/250 g/1⅓ cup brown sugar
1 lb/500 g/2½ cup mixed fruit: sultanas, currants,
raisins and cherries
4 eggs
2 oz/50 g/½ cup grated cheddar cheese
6-8 tbsp /120-160 ml milk
salt

Sift flour, salt and sugar. Rub in the dripping. Add cheese and fruit. Make a well in the mixture and add beaten eggs and milk. Bake in a well-greased log tin for about 1¾ hrs at gas mark 4-5/300°F/150°C.

Bara mel Sinsir

Honey Gingerbread

Welsh gingerbread was sold at fairs. The original gingerbread had no ginger in it but tasted as if it did.

---

6 oz / 200 g / 1½ cups self-raising flour
pinch bicarbonate of soda
pinch ground ginger
pinch nutmeg
3 oz / 90 g / ½ cup brown sugar
6 oz / 175 g / ½ cup honey
¼ pint / 125 ml / ½ cup water
5 oz / 140 g / ¼ cup butter

Mix dry ingredients together. Put honey, water and butter in a saucepan. Stir over a low heat until the butter is just melted. Add to dry ingredients. Mix well. Pour into a very well-greased flat square tin and bake for about ¾ hour at gas mark 4-5 / 350°F / 150°C. Cool in tin. Cut into squares, dust with icing sugar, and decorate each square with a small piece of preserved ginger.

Cage Bach

Welsh Cakes

These small cakes are to Wales as barmcakes are to
Scotland. They were made and served at Sunday teatime
and if there were any left over they were given to the
miners in their 'tocyn'. *Cage Bach* were made on the
griddlestone – one of the Welsh cook's basic cooking
utensils.

½ lb/250 g/2 cups self-raising flour
¼ lb/125 g/½ cup butter
¼ lb/125 g/½ cup sugar
¼ lb/125 g/⅔ cup sultanas
pinch cinnamon
1 large egg, beaten

Rub flour, butter and sugar to fine crumbs. Add spice.
Make a well in the centre, then add egg and fruit. Mix to a
firm dough, roll out to ¼ in/¾ cm thick, and cut into
rounds. Cook on a heated griddle or heavy fryingpan until
brown on both sides. Cool and spread with butter before
eating.

Pwdin Mynwy

Monmouth Pudding

This recipe was given to me by an old lady who had been a young parlour maid on the Thomas Johnes' Hafod estate. The Hafod estate was a haven for rich and famous artists and writers. William Turner regularly visited the Johnes family.

½ lb/250 g/4 cups fresh white breadcrumbs
4 egg yolks
1½ oz/30 g butter
2 oz/50 g caster sugar
¾ pint/450 ml/1¾ cups milk
rind of two lemons
red jam

Add the lemon rind, sugar and butter to the milk. Bring to the boil and allow to cool. Add eggs and pour over breadcrumbs. Grease a pudding basin, pour in half the mixture then add the jam in the centre then the rest of the mixture. Bake at gas mark 4-5/300°F/150°C for about ¾ hour or until set.

Crempog

Pancakes

Crempog is the original Welsh pancake. It was often served for breakfast in Wales in the eighteenth century. Now it is a popular teatime treat.

---

5 oz/175 g/1¼ cup self-raising flour
2 oz/65 g/¼ cup white sugar
4 tbsp/80 ml sour milk
1 tsp bicarbonate of soda
4 small eggs
10 tbsp/200 ml milk
2 tbsp cream of tartar
large knob of melted butter

Put all the dry ingredients into a large bowl. Add milk, eggs and butter and mix thoroughly. Cook in tablespoonfuls on a greased, hot, heavy fryingpan and serve hot with butter and honey.

Savouries

Welsh Rarebit
Possibly the most famous of all Welsh dishes although how it came by its name has been lost to history. This is one of many variations.

½ lb/250 g/2 cups stale cheese, grated	1 tsp dry mustard
4 tbsp stout or beer	2 tsp flour
knob of butter	salt and pepper
	slices of toast

Make a *roux* with the butter and flour. Season. Add liquid, cheese and mustard and mix well. Spread on slices of toast and grill until brown.

Bara Laver (Laver Bread)

A visit to Wales would not be complete without tasting laver bread which is made with seaweed and oatmeal. It is readily available in most markets in Dyfed. If you make it yourself, wash the seaweed well. Boil for several hours until it is quite soft. Drain and season. Mix well with enough fine oatmeal to make small round cakes. Fry in bacon fat and serve with bacon and Glamorgan sausages for breakfast.

Stwmp

I think every home in Wales has a variation on this dish. This is the one I know and still love to eat.

8 large potatoes	2 big knobs butter
4 large carrots	salt and pepper
½ small swede	

Peel and chop the vegetables. Cook until soft. Mash well with the butter. Season. Serve piping hot.

Teisienau Sir Fon

Anglesey Cakes

It was customary in times past for children in Anglesey to receive these little cakes when they went 'first footing' to wish their neighbours a Happy New Year. The children would sing the following verse as a thank you.

> Calennig yn gyfan,
> Mae heddiw'n Ddydd Calan,
> Unwaith, dwywaith, tri.
> Blwyddyn Newydd Dda i chi

which, loosely translated, means:

> Today is New Year's Day
> And we wish you
> Once, twice, three times,
> A very happy New Year.

¾ lb/420 g/3 cups self-raising flour
¼ lb/25 g/½ cup caster sugar
½ lb/250 g/1 cup unsalted butter
red jam
icing sugar

Warm the butter but do not let it melt. Mix in the sugar and work in the flour. Roll out fairly thin. Cut into 2 in/5 cm rounds. Bake in gas mark 4/300°F/180°C oven for about 10 minutes until golden brown in colour. When cool, sandwich the rounds together and dowse in icing sugar.

Cyflaith

Toffee

Cyflaith was another sweet that was given to the children who went 'Hela Calennig' or first footing in the New Year.

¾ lb/370 g/2 cups brown sugar
¼ lb/125 g/½ cup unsalted butter
2 tbsp golden syrup
(treacle may be used if a darker toffee is preferred)
3 tbsp water
dash of rum
handful of chopped almonds

Put all the ingredients, apart from the nuts, into a heavy saucepan and heat on low until butter has melted and sugar dissolved. Bring to the boil and cook for 10-15 minutes or until some of the toffee hardens when dropped into a cup of cold water. Add the nuts and pour into a well-greased flat square tin and score in squares before it hardens. Leave to cool and then break into small pieces.

Drinks

Elderflower Wine
Elderflower grows by the sides of the lanes in Wales and

makes an easy and very cheap wine. Quite often it was served at early nineteenth century weddings.

---

8 heads of elderflowers
2 lemons
1½ lb/750 g/3 cups white sugar
1 gallon/4¾ ltrs cold water
2 tbsp white wine vinegar

Boil the water and cool. Add the sugar, elderflower heads, lemon juice and rind, and vinegar. Leave for 24 hours, then strain, bottle and cork. This is a beautiful, fizzy wine.

Ginger Beer

This is a drink made at harvest time; it is cheap and easy to make and very potent. It used to be kept in stone bottles, but will keep equally well in modern glass ones.

---

2 gallons/9½ ltrs water
juice and peel of 3 lemons
1 oz/25 g yeast
1 ginger root
4 oz/125 g/⅔ cup raisins
2½ lbs/1¼ kg/5 cups sugar
pinch cream tartar

Cut the ginger in pieces and put in a pan with the juice and peel of the lemons, sugar, raisins, and cream of tartar. Pour the boiling water over and when cool add the yeast. Put liquid into a large clean pot and stir well. Stand in a warm place. Skim off the yeast, lemon peel, and raisins.

Strain liquid into another clean pot. Bottle and leave to stand for three days before drinking. Cork lightly to begin with as bottles may burst if corked too tightly.

Te Scota
This was a favourite drink of the fishermen who took the boats out of Newquay in Dyfed when the mists hung low. It probably helped to keep the chill winds at bay.

2 parts gin	1 part treacle

Mix the ingredients together and drink slowly.

Gaffo
In Cornwall this drink is called a shandy gabby, in Ireland a porter gabb.

1 part beer	1 part ginger beer

Mix well. Serve chilled.

Oggyot
Oggyot, an alcoholic egg flip, was given to women, especially nursing mothers, and children were given it to thicken their blood. Most often, however, it was drunk as a nightcap. It certainly tastes delicious.

½ pint / 300 ml / 1¼ cup milk	2 tbsp rum
2 eggs	1 tbsp sugar

Beat the eggs, heat the milk almost to boiling, add sugar and rum. Whisk all together and drink while hot.

Index